PLANES
ROCKETS —and other—
FLYING MACHINES

Author:

Ian Graham was born in Belfast in 1953. He studied applied physics at The City University, London, and earned a postgraduate diploma in journalism at the same university, specializing in science and technology journalism. After four years as an editor of consumer electronics magazines, he became a freelance author and journalist. Since then, he has written more than one hundred children's nonfiction books and numerous magazine articles.

Artist:

Nick Hewetson was born in Surrey, England, in 1958. He was educated in Sussex at Brighton Technical School, and studied illustration at Eastbourne College of Art. He has illustrated a wide variety of children's books.

Editor:

Tanya Kant

Editorial Assistant:

Mark Williams

This edition first published in 2014 by Book House

Distributed by Black Rabbit Books
P.O. Box 3263
Mankato
Minnesota MN 56002

 SALARIYA

© 2014 The Salariya Book Company Ltd

Printed in the United States of America.
Printed on paper from sustainable forests.

Cataloging-in-Publication Data is available from the Library of Congress

ISBN: 978-1-908973-95-5

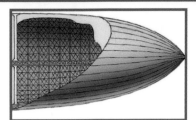

PLANES
ROCKETS —and other—
FLYING MACHINES

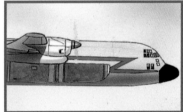

Written by
IAN GRAHAM

Illustrated by
NICK HEWETSON

Created and designed by
DAVID SALARIYA

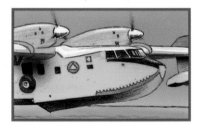

BOOK HOUSE
a SALARIYA *imprint*

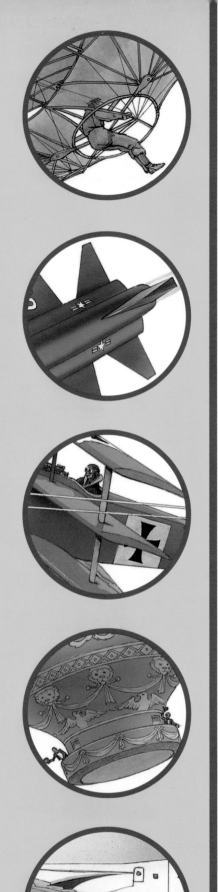

Contents

Dreams of Flight

▶ A 15th-century flying machine, designed by Leonardo da Vinci.

Early flying machines failed because they tried to copy the flapping action of a bird's wings. Things changed with the development of fixed-wing gliders in the 18th century. In 1903, the Wright brothers added an engine and **propellers** to their glider—they created the first airplane, the *Flyer*.

▲ *Birds fly in a different way from airplanes.*

▼ *In 1849, one of George Cayley's gliders carried the weight of a boy. In 1853 his last glider carried a man across an English valley.*

Cayley's 1853 glider

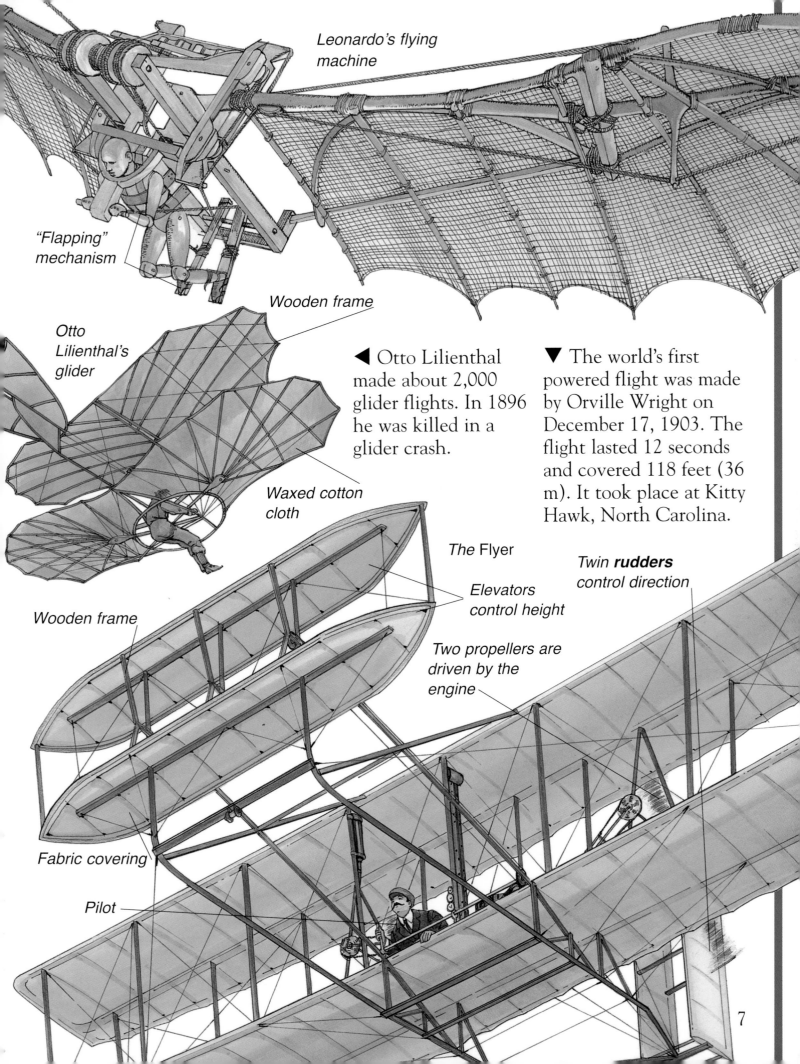

Leonardo's flying machine

"Flapping" mechanism

Otto Lilienthal's glider

Wooden frame

Waxed cotton cloth

◀ Otto Lilienthal made about 2,000 glider flights. In 1896 he was killed in a glider crash.

▼ The world's first powered flight was made by Orville Wright on December 17, 1903. The flight lasted 12 seconds and covered 118 feet (36 m). It took place at Kitty Hawk, North Carolina.

The Flyer

Elevators control height

Twin **rudders** control direction

Two propellers are driven by the engine

Wooden frame

Fabric covering

Pilot

▶ John Alcock and Arthur Whitten Brown made the first nonstop transatlantic flight in 1919. They flew a World War I Vickers Vimy.

Vickers Vimy

Trailblazers

The history of powered flight is full of brave pioneers and record-breaking routes. Military needs and competition between **aviation** companies have led to new inventions such as **jet engines**, **radar**, and rocket planes.

Spirit of St Louis

▲ May 20, 1927: The *Spirit of St. Louis* flew from New York to Paris in 33 hours and 39 minutes. Pilot Charles Lindbergh was the first person to fly solo and nonstop across the North Atlantic Ocean.

▼ 1924: Two Douglas World Cruisers made the first around-the-world flight. It took 175 days, with 72 stops.

Douglas World Cruiser

Rutan and Yeager's plane, Voyager

N26SVA

▲ 1986: Dick Rutan and Jeana Yeager made the first nonstop, around-the-world flight in just 9 days.

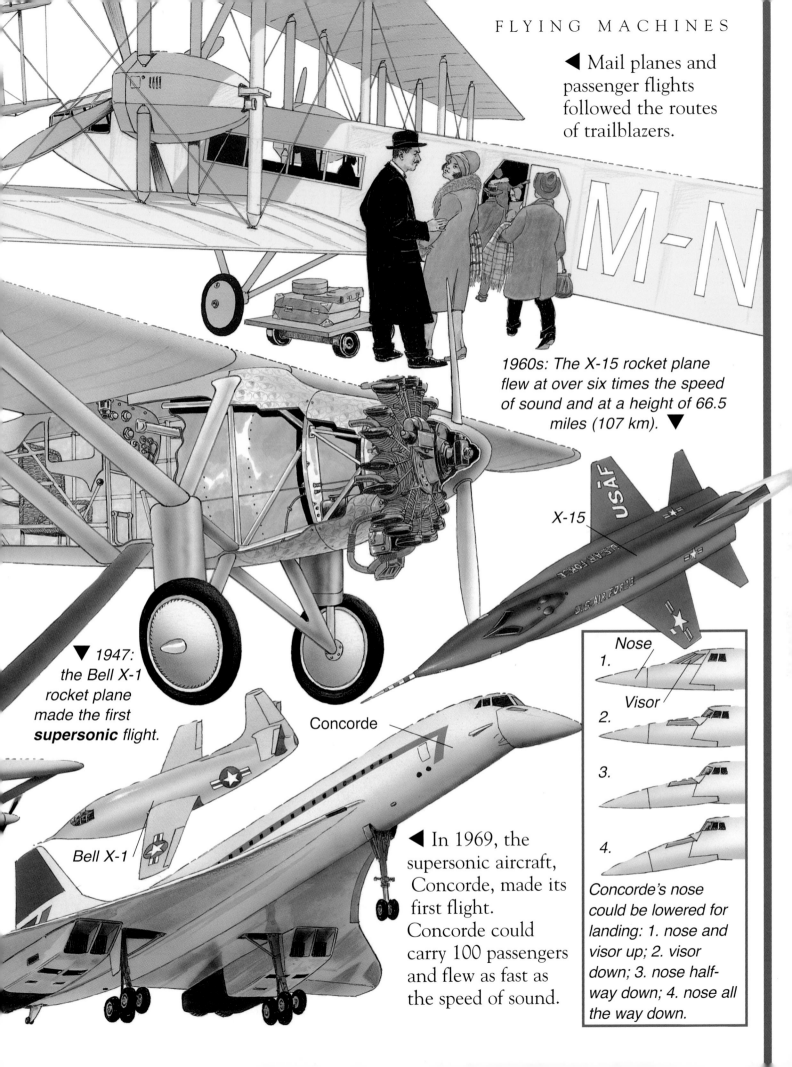

◀ Mail planes and passenger flights followed the routes of trailblazers.

1960s: The X-15 rocket plane flew at over six times the speed of sound and at a height of 66.5 miles (107 km). ▼

X-15

▼ 1947: the Bell X-1 rocket plane made the first **supersonic** flight.

Bell X-1

Concorde

◀ In 1969, the supersonic aircraft, Concorde, made its first flight. Concorde could carry 100 passengers and flew as fast as the speed of sound.

Nose

1.

Visor

2.

3.

4.

Concorde's nose could be lowered for landing: 1. nose and visor up; 2. visor down; 3. nose half-way down; 4. nose all the way down.

Planes for War

Airplanes first went to war during World War I. If a plane started to drop bombs then other planes were sent to fight it. World War II fighter planes could exceed 300 miles per hour, or "mph" (480 km/h). By the end of the war, **jet fighters** were introduced. Bombers, fighters and **stealth planes** are used in combat today.

Fokker Triplane

▼ Sopwith Camels were armed with machine guns and flew at about 125 mph (200 km/h).

Sopwith Camel

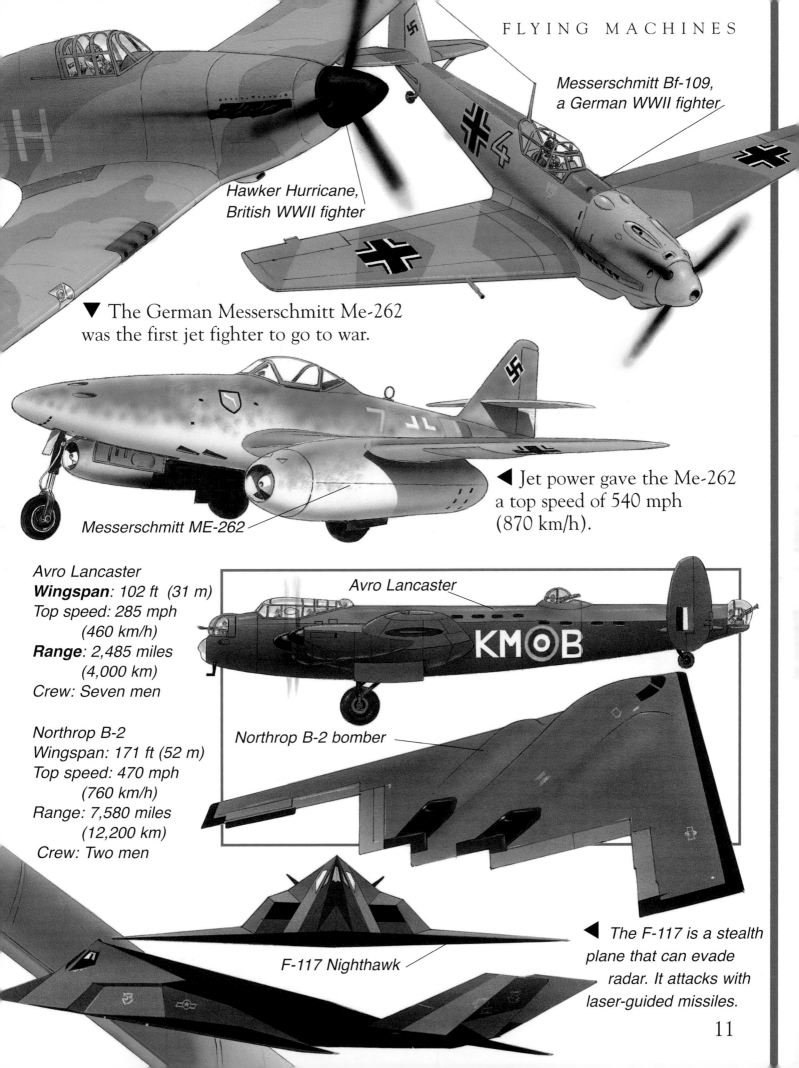

Messerschmitt Bf-109, a German WWII fighter

Hawker Hurricane, British WWII fighter

▼ The German Messerschmitt Me-262 was the first jet fighter to go to war.

◄ Jet power gave the Me-262 a top speed of 540 mph (870 km/h).

Messerschmitt ME-262

Avro Lancaster
Wingspan: 102 ft (31 m)
Top speed: 285 mph
(460 km/h)
Range: 2,485 miles
(4,000 km)
Crew: Seven men

Avro Lancaster

Northrop B-2
Wingspan: 171 ft (52 m)
Top speed: 470 mph
(760 km/h)
Range: 7,580 miles
(12,200 km)
Crew: Two men

Northrop B-2 bomber

F-117 Nighthawk

◄ The F-117 is a stealth plane that can evade radar. It attacks with laser-guided missiles.

Balloons and Airships

The first manned flight was made in a hot-air balloon. It used hot air to float upward.

Hot-air balloons rise because the hot air inside them is lighter than the air that surrounds them.

The Hindenburg
Launched: 1936
Length: 804 ft (245 m)
Width: 135 ft (41 m)

D-LZ129

Passenger decks

Engines

▼ *In 1783, the first manned hot-air balloon flight carried two men for 25 minutes.*

Hot-air balloons travel wherever the wind blows them. Airships can be steered.

Montgolfier balloon

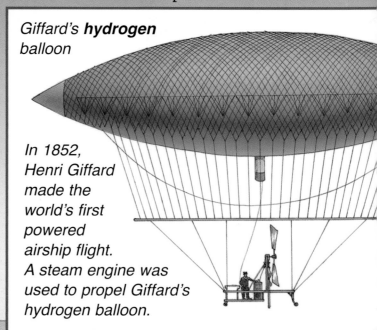

Giffard's **hydrogen** *balloon*

In 1852, Henri Giffard made the world's first powered airship flight. A steam engine was used to propel Giffard's hydrogen balloon.

German Zeppelins were filled with hydrogen gas. Hydrogen is the lightest gas of all, so it allowed the Zeppelins to lift a large weight. Hydrogen is a dangerous gas because it is highly flammable.

◀ On May 6, 1937, the *Hindenburg* caught fire as it approached its mooring mast during an electrical storm. It only took 34 seconds for the entire airship to catch fire. Amazingly, 62 of its 97 passengers and crew managed to escape.

Fabric covering

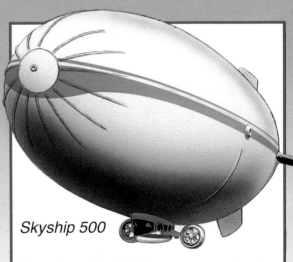

Skyship 500

The Skyship 500 is a modern airship. It is filled with safe helium gas and propelled by two Porsche car engines. It carries up to ten people.

15

Special Planes

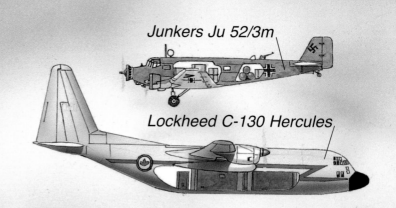

Junkers Ju 52/3m

Lockheed C-130 Hercules

Planes have many uses beyond carrying passengers. They can be used to spray crops, fight fires, carry cargo, work as air ambulances, and even compete in contests.

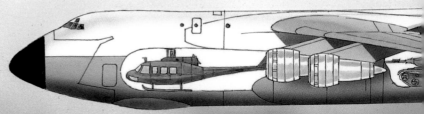

▲ Cargo planes are built with lots of space to carry goods in.

Flight deck

Shorts S23 flying boat

Seaplanes and **flying boats** can land on water.

Bell UH-1 Iroquois

CH-47 Chinook

▲ Helicopters were used to transport US troops and cargo during the Vietnam War (1965–1975).

Cargo

▲ The Boeing Vertol CH-47 Chinook could transport 40 troops or 8 tons of cargo.

The McDonnell Douglas AH-64 Apache is designed to attack armored vehicles, such as tanks.

Missile launcher

Machine gun

Airliners

The first passenger airliners were often converted warplanes. They were unreliable, cold, and noisy. But air travel became popular during the 1930s, so true passenger airliners like the Boeing 247 were introduced.

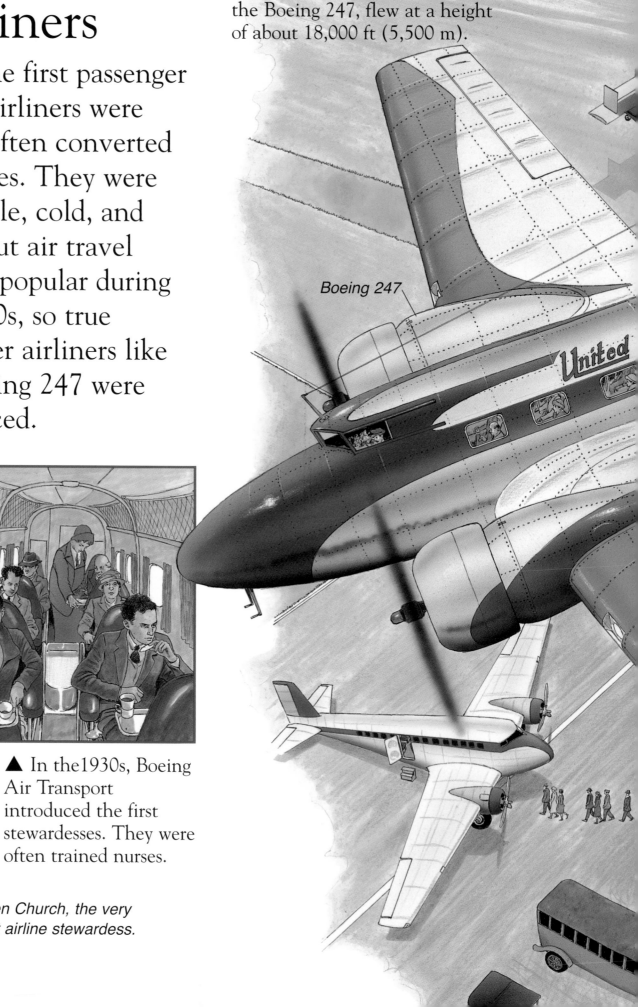

▼ The first modern airliner, the Boeing 247, flew at a height of about 18,000 ft (5,500 m).

Boeing 247

United

▲ In the 1930s, Boeing Air Transport introduced the first stewardesses. They were often trained nurses.

Ellen Church, the very first airline stewardess.

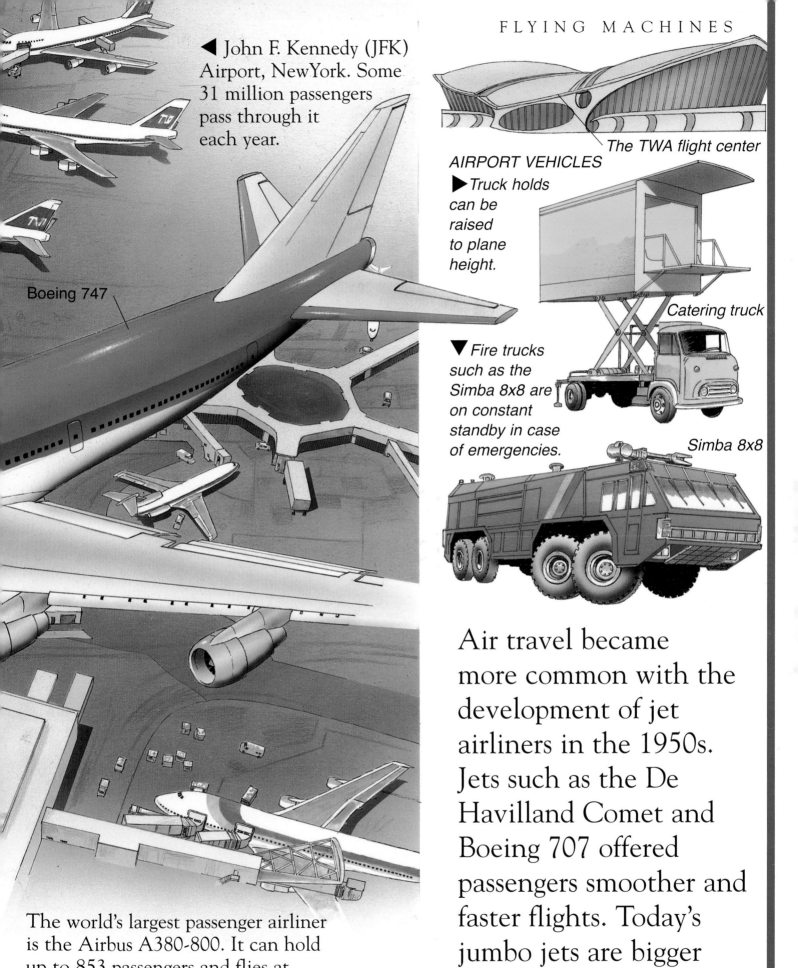

◀ John F. Kennedy (JFK) Airport, New York. Some 31 million passengers pass through it each year.

The TWA flight center

Boeing 747

AIRPORT VEHICLES

▶Truck holds can be raised to plane height.

Catering truck

▼ Fire trucks such as the Simba 8x8 are on constant standby in case of emergencies.

Simba 8x8

The world's largest passenger airliner is the Airbus A380-800. It can hold up to 853 passengers and flies at around 560 mph (900 km/h).

Air travel became more common with the development of jet airliners in the 1950s. Jets such as the De Havilland Comet and Boeing 707 offered passengers smoother and faster flights. Today's jumbo jets are bigger and faster than ever.

25

Spacecraft

On October 4, 1957, *Sputnik 1* was blasted into **orbit**. It was the world's first man-made **satellite**. In 1961, the Soviet Union (Russia) launched the first man into space. In 1969, men first landed on the moon in the US *Apollo 11* spacecraft.

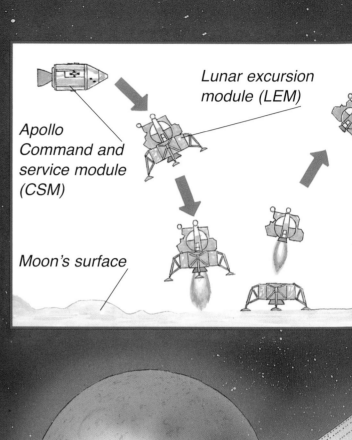

Apollo Command and service module (CSM)

Lunar excursion module (LEM)

Moon's surface

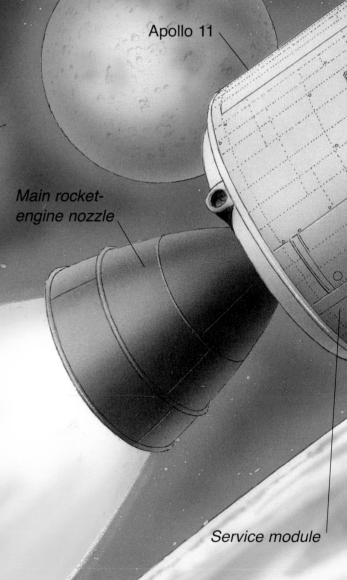

Apollo 11

Main rocket-engine nozzle

Service module

Yuri Gagarin

Vostok 1

▲ The first person to travel into space was Yuri Gagarin. He made an orbit of the Earth in *Vostok 1*.

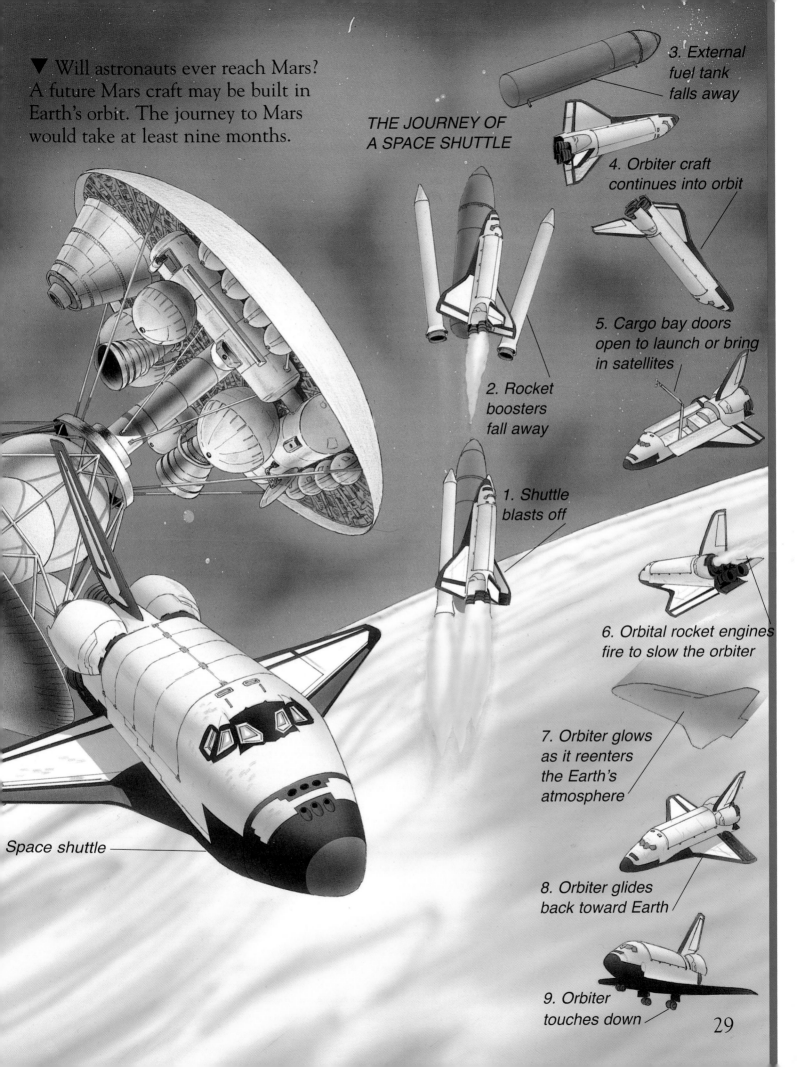

▼ Will astronauts ever reach Mars? A future Mars craft may be built in Earth's orbit. The journey to Mars would take at least nine months.

THE JOURNEY OF A SPACE SHUTTLE

3. External fuel tank falls away

4. Orbiter craft continues into orbit

5. Cargo bay doors open to launch or bring in satellites

2. Rocket boosters fall away

1. Shuttle blasts off

6. Orbital rocket engines fire to slow the orbiter

7. Orbiter glows as it reenters the Earth's atmosphere

8. Orbiter glides back toward Earth

9. Orbiter touches down

Space shuttle

Useful Words

Aviation
Another word for flying.

Flying boat
An airplane with a boat-shaped body and floats under its wings so that it can land on water.

Hydrogen
A flammable gas that is lighter than air.

Jet engine
An aircraft engine that forces a stream of hot gases out through an opening at the rear of the engine.

Jet fighter
A military airplane powered by one or more jet engines.

Orbit
The path a satellite or spacecraft follows as it circles a planet.

Propellers
Angled blades that spin to pull a plane through the air.

Radar
Stands for RAdio Detection And Ranging. A system for locating objects that are too far away to see. It works by bouncing radio waves off them and measuring the time for the reflected waves to return.

Range
The maximum distance an aircraft can fly without having to refuel.

Rotor
A set of rotating blades on a helicopter.

Rudder
A panel in an aircraft's tail fin. The pilot swivels it to turn the aircraft left or right.

Satellite
An object, such as a spacecraft or a moon, that orbits another object, such as a planet.

Seaplane
An airplane that can land on water.

Stealth plane
A warplane that is made to be difficult for enemy radar systems to find. Its shape stops the enemy's radar waves from being reflected back strongly.

Supersonic
Faster than the speed of sound.

Thermal
A column of warm air that rises from the Earth.

Wingspan
The distance between a plane's wingtips.

Zeppelin
A type of airship with a rigid frame.

Milestones

1783 November The first manned flight is made in a Montgolfier hot-air balloon in Paris.

1903 The Wright brothers make the first powered, controlled flight in an airplane.

1926 Robert Goddard launches the first liquid-fueled rocket.

1939 Igor Sikorsky designs the first practical and successful helicopter, the VS-300.

1947 Charles "Chuck" Yeager makes the first supersonic flight in the Bell X-1 experimental rocket plane.

1952 The first jet airliner, the De Havilland Comet, enters service.

1957 October *Sputnik 1*, launched by the Soviet Union, is the world's first artificial satellite.

1961 April Yuri Gagarin is the first human being to leave Earth and travel into space.

1962 February John Glenn becomes the first US astronaut to orbit the Earth, in his *Friendship 7* Mercury capsule.

1968 December Human beings circle the moon for the first time—the crew of *Apollo 8*.

1969 February The Boeing 747 jumbo jet makes its first flight.

1969 March The supersonic airliner Concorde makes its first flight.

1969 July Neil Armstrong is the first person to walk on the moon, closely followed by Edwin "Buzz" Aldrin, while Michael Collins circles the moon. They are the crew of *Apollo 11*.

1970 December The Soviet Union lands the first space probe, *Venera 7*, on the surface of Venus.

1971 The Soviet space station *Salyut 1* is launched.

1976 January The supersonic airliner Concorde enters service.

1977 *Voyager 1* and *Voyager 2* launch on their tour of the solar system.

1986 February The Soviet Union launches the *Mir* space station.

2008 May The *Phoenix* probe successfully lands on Mars.

2008 August Scott Kasprowicz and Steve Sheik set a new record for the fastest around-the-world helicopter flight: 11 days and 7 hours.

Index